Puddlejumpers

The Keytext Program

Louise Matteoni
Wilson H. Lane
Floyd Sucher
Thomas D. Yawkey

Theodore L. Harris, Advisory Author

Harold B. Allen, Linguistic Consultant

THE ECONOMY COMPANY

Oklahoma City   Indianapolis   Orange, CA

The Keytext Program was developed with the participation of Kraft and Kraft, Stow, Massachusetts.

Design and Art Direction: James Stockton

Cover Illustration: Pat Maloney

Permission to use or adapt copyright material appearing in this book is gratefully acknowledged on page 160, which is hereby made a part of this copyright page.

ISBN 0-8332-1030-0

THE ECONOMY COMPANY, Educational Publishers
1901 North Walnut   Oklahoma City, Oklahoma 73125

Contents

The Land of Hop

Don and Jean in the Land of Hop

	We work with words.		Sound the words.

We work with words.　　　　Sound the words.

dog	hit	hug	hop
duck	Fred	fog	from
teeth	mean	Eve	Jean
hit	hot	band	Don
list	hug	left	land
trip	shop	paint	top
flea	flown	flour	flat

8

Ride to Hop

"Come, read this," said Jean.
"Come to the Land of Hop!
Have fun!
See our grass grow!"

"Let's do it, Jean," said Don.
"Let's go to the Land of Hop."

"I like it here," said Jean.
"And we have no way to get there."

"But you do," said a big frog.
"I'm Green Frog.
I'm on my way to the Land of Hop.
Come fly with me."

And they did.

9

"We will land soon," said Green Frog.
"I can see the top of Hop City.
You can stay at the Top of the Hop.
It is a good place to stay.
Here is a book you will need.
It will help you talk in Hop Talk.
See? Here is how to say that the
water is not good.
Have fun in the Land of Hop!
I must go look for a job here.
I'll be back for you soon.
Then I'll take you from here
to Flat Bend."

10

"Look," said Jean.
"Here come the Hop people.
Look at them hop!"

"Quick, Jean!" said Don.
"Say we are from Flat Bend.
We want to see the grass grow.
Say it in Hop Talk."

"You don't need to," the Hop
people said.
"We talk like you.
But we don't have grass.
We just have ice and a
Rock Monster.
You may hop and slide on
the ice.
But not on top of the
Rock Monster.
He does not like it."

11

We work with words.   Sound the word.

fry   sky   by

Sight words.

"<u>Oh</u>, no! I <u>think</u> it's a monster."

The Rock Monster

Don and Jean went to slide on ice.

Then Jean said, "Let's stop!

My feet feel as if they will

freeze off.

Let's slide on that big rock, Don."

"Oh!" The big rock let out a howl.

"Stop that!"

"You must be the Rock Monster,"

said Don.

12

"Yes, I am," the Rock Monster
said.

"The people here don't like me.
They don't think it is good
for me to hop.

And they don't come by me.
Will you hop with me?"

Don and Jean did hop with it.
Hop! Hop! Hop!

"I want to go back to Flat Bend,"
said Jean.

"Oh! Good!" said the Rock Monster.
"Will you take me with you?"

"I think you are too big," said Don.

"I can fix that," said the Rock
Monster.

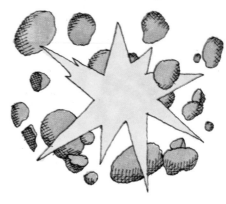

"Oh! Now you are little," said Jean.
"Now you can go with us."

Just then Green Frog came by for them.
"Let's go!" he said.
14   And they all went home to Flat Bend.

Lost and Found

Lost in the Sky

We work with words.

blade bless blown

please plain plate

plums legs takes

skip ask skin

miss sand west

Sound the words.

blow

plane

planes

sky

wind

Sight words.

Were you lost?

16

The Little Plane

"Do not go, little plane," the big planes said.

"Soon it will rain.

The sky will be black.

You will get lost in the sky.

Stay home, little plane."

"I will not stay home," said the little plane.

"You are big and I am little.

But I can fly fast.

I like the rain.

Let the sky get black!

I will not get lost!"

17

"Here I go!" said the little plane.

"What fun I will have.

Let the sky get black.

Let it rain.

I will go, go, go!

It can rain all day.

It can rain all night.

But it will not stop me!

"Let the big planes stay home,"
said the little plane.

"Let them stay on the ground.

They were not like me.

I will not be like them.

I will fly and fly.

Here I come, sky."

19

"Yes! Here you come," said the wind.

"You were here to go this way
and that.

But you will not go the way you
want to go.

You will go the way I blow you.

Go, little plane!

Go as I blow."

"No!" said the little plane.

"If I go the way you blow, I will
get lost.

I do not want to get lost
in the sky."

"I have you now!" said the wind.

How the wind did blow!
How the wind did howl!
The little plane went fast.
But it went the way of the wind.

"Help!" said the little plane.
"I do not want to go this way."

21

"Let me go, wind!" said the little plane.

"Let me go my way.

You will make me get lost.

I can get back to the ground, now.

But soon I will be lost.

I will be lost in the sky.

Stop, wind, stop!

Let me go!"

But the wind did not stop.

We work with words.

free	fruit	fresh
trick	trade	trap
ball	tall	wall
ten	egg	send
best	star	mast
mow	row	tow

Sound the words.

froze

trip

fall

end

rest

low

Sight word..

I <u>knew</u> you were lost.

Fly from the Wind

"Little plane," said the wind,

"this is the end of you.

You will freeze and fall.

You can't make the trip home now."

"The big planes said not to go," said the little plane.

"But I still went.

I said to let it rain.

I said to let the sky get black.

I knew I was fast!

But I can't go my way.

The big planes are at home.

But I am lost in the sky.

I may freeze and fall.

Will it be the end of me?"

24

The little plane did not see
the way home.

The rain froze on it.

The wind did not stop.

"I said to let it rain,"
the little plane said.

"But the rain froze on me.

The rain froze to ice.

I need to rest.

But I can't rest.

I must not fall!

I will try to go down.

If I fly low, the wind can't
blow me.

I will fly low, down by the
ground.

Soon this trip will end.

Then I can rest."

25

"The wind did blow me," said the
little plane.
"The rain froze on me.
But I can see the way home.
I am not lost now.
Soon I can rest!"

"Little plane!" the big planes said.
"We just knew you were lost."

"I was lost in the ice and wind,"
the little plane said.
"Next time you tell me not to go,
I will not go at all."

Always a Happy Ending

Is It a Duck Egg?

We work with words.

Jack   lack   sock

tag   team   wet

yeast   yap   yam

miss   fill   muff

Sound the words.

duck

tail

yet

egg

Sight word.

Were you the <u>one</u>?

28

The Last Egg

A duck egg is a duck egg.

But is it?

This is B. J. Duck.

This is a B. J. Duck egg.

And this is a B. J. Duck egg.

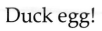

And this is a B. J. Duck egg.

Yet this does not look like a B. J.
Duck egg!

Does it, B. J. Duck?

29

"Well, no," said B. J. Duck.

"This egg is good.

And this egg is good.

And this egg is good.

But this one, well, you can't

30   win them all."

Out they come, one by one.

They jump out feet first. Jump!

And tail first. Bump!

Tail and feet first,

out they all come.

No! Wait! That one, that big one,

is not here yet!

31

"Oh, come on!" said a little duck.
"We are all here but you!
We want to line up in a little line
and slide in the water!
We can't wait all day!
Come on, you in the egg!
Let's get on with it!"

stack   stick   trick

sky   mask   skin

noun   round   shout

beat   nail   life

quack

ask

found

fine

Sight word.

The <u>swan</u> is in the water.

Not as a Duck

He didn't look like a little duck.

He did not sound like a little duck.

"QUAAAK!!!!"

"I must ask you not to make a quack
sound like that again," said B. J. Duck.

"QUAAAAK!!!!"

"Now," said B. J. Duck.
"Let's take it from the top again.
Say, 'quack.'
Make it sound like this. 'Quack'!"

"QUAAAAAK!!!!"

"I don't think you will make it
as a duck," said B. J. Duck.
    "A duck must quack well."

34

But he didn't quack well.

He didn't look good.

And he didn't fly at all.

No little duck came to ask him
to play.

No little duck came to talk
to him.

They all found a way to make fun of him.

And so he found it went, day in
and day out.

Then one day he got a good look at
the duck in the water.

But did he?

It was not a duck he found.

"Well, I'll be a swan," he said.
"Oh! I think I am a swan."

He still can't fly.

And he still can't quack.

But a swan does not have to.

Now they all come and ask him to play.

B. J. Duck still does not think

he can make it as a duck.

But that is fine with her.

It is fine with him, too.

The Job Shop

The Toy Shop

We work with words.

soil	paint	join
	boy	joy
tall	Tom	tail
bags	legs	boys
raise	these	those
band	hid	hot
bird	term	fur
cheese	keep	steel

Sound the words.

oil

Roy

toy

toys

noise

shop

girl

needs

Sight word.

<u>Rosa</u> has a toy duck.

Roy had to get a toy.

He had to get it for Rosa.

He went in to get the toy.

He said to the woman,

"I need a toy for Rosa.

She likes loud noise!"

The woman said to the man,

"He wants a toy that will make noise."

The woman went to the back.

She came from the back of the
shop with a big toy.

She said, "I may have just
what the girl likes.
But it needs oil.
The oil needs to go in the hole.
It will make a noise like a loud howl!"

Roy said, "Is this a toy for a girl?"

The woman said, "Toys are toys."

Rosa did use the oil.
She did make the truck go fast.

"Oh! What a noise," Rosa said.

Rosa said, "I like this truck.

Now I want to get a toy for Roy."

She went to the Toy Shop.

To the man she said, "You have toys.

Roy needs a toy.

He does not like noise."

The shop man got down a toy duck

and said, "It does not make noise."

"Will Roy like it?" the girl said.

"What do you think?" the man said.

"Yes. He will like it," Rosa said.

And Roy did.

We Work with Words

We work with words.   Sound the words.

mud   hum   mail   mom

thin   path   third   these

worm   worst   word

girls   works   makes   words

worth   world   work

storm   corn   horn   or

Sight word.

Use <u>more</u> words, Bob.

42

Nan and her mom like to play a game with words.

Nan has a box for her words.

She went to look for words in her box.

"Mom! Mom!" she said.

"My words! Look!

Can you fix this word?

Can you fix this word, too?"

"No, I can't," her mom said.

"But don't feel blue.

We will go to the Word Shop.

They fix words at the Word Shop."

A woman said, "May I help you?"

"Yes," Nan said.
"I need you to fix these words.
I need them to play a game.
Can you fix these words?"

"Do you see these words?" she said.
"If you look at these, you will
see I can fix words.
What do you want this word to be?"

"That word is flat, or eat," said Nan.
"You see! I can't tell.
I will use it with this word.
Will you fix it, too?"

"In this shop, words are our work,"
the woman said.
"I will work on these words.
You can look at more words

44   if you like."

Nan and her mom went to look at all the words in the shop.

"Say!" Nan said.

"Here are more words!

We can look at more big words or little words.

We can look at play words or sound words.

Mom, can you read all these words?"

Her mom said, "Yes, I can.

And soon you will read them, too." 45

"Here you are," the woman said.
"Your words are eat and time."

"Eat and time!" said Mom.
"Soon it will be time for us
to eat, Nan!" Mom said.

"Wait!" said Nan.
"You can have the word eat.
I will take this one."

"Game?" said Mom.
"That is a good word, too."

"Yes," said Nan.
"Game and Time make Game Time.
Let's go play our word game."
And they did.

A Dog's Tale

How to Wash
a Big Dog

We work with words.   Sound the words.

walk   wall   want   wash

ran   hid   Ben   dog

sea   bike   gave   nose

round   count   flour   shout

looks   takes   plants   its

tag   wax   band   wag

48

Do you have a big dog?

Here is how to wash a big dog.

It's good if you have a friend help you.

You will need help!

Do as I tell you.

1. Don't say "water" or "wash" to the dog.

If you do, it will hide.

2. The dog may try to run.

Get the dog and don't let go.

3. You take the tail end.

Your friend may take the nose end.

Make the dog stand in the water.

Try to get all of it in the water.

4. Try not to let the water fly out.

It will make you slip and slide and fall.

5. The dog will jump and duck.

It will jerk and howl and may growl.

But don't let go.

6. You may shout.

Shout "Down, dog! Down!"

If that does not work, shout "Stop it!"

The dog may not stop.

Still, don't let go.

7. Now wash its nose.

Wash its tail.

Wash all of the dog.

The dog may not like it.

But it will be good for the dog.

8. Now let the dog out of the water.

Its tail will wag.

9. Now the dog needs to eat.

Its tail will wag and wag and wag!

Samson, the Dog

We work with words.

Sound the words.

paint	pay	map		paw
	cause	fault		sauce
law	raw	yawn		saw
bike	band	best		boy
sea	send	side		so
hot	hid	send		tag
Eve	hope	trade		goat
bloom	noon	root		zoo

Sight words.

Samson, run from the bear!

51

My name is Samson.

I'm a big black dog.

I have one brown paw.

I stay with a boy and a girl.

We play tag and have fun.

But if they try to wash me, I hide.

Then they call, "Samson! Samson!

Come here."

But I don't come.

I don't want to go in that water!

If I can get out, I run to the zoo.

I look at the bear.

One time I found a black goat.

I saw the fish play tag.

I saw a duck, too.

I like to look at the bear, the goat, the fish, and the duck in the zoo.

I like the zoo.

It's a good place to hide.

Oh! Oh! Look out!

It's him again!

And them again! Oh, no!

A bear and a goat I can stand.

But not them!

It is bad like this again and again as I try to run off and hide!

53

I hide if they look for me.

It's no fun to be in that water.

It's not like a game of tag!

I hide under my big paw.

I'm just a dog!

I like to play.

I like to eat.

I like my home.

54 But I don't like them to wash me!

I want to play tag with them
and then eat.

But if I go home, they may say
I'm a bad dog.

So I sit by the street.

One paw is under me.

One paw is on the curb.

It's not a good day for me.

I do not want them to wash me.

But now I need it.

And I do want to eat.

At home, I can have sauce from a can.

It's so good!

It's no fun to hide all day.

I like my home.

I like the boy and the girl.

I like the big can with the sauce.

So I get up and go home.

I go by the zoo and down the street.

Then I'm home.

"Samson! Samson!" they say.

"It is so good to see you again!"

I wag my tail.

It's good to be home.

I will eat first.

The sauce is so good!

They will wash me, but it will

not be so bad.

The Perfect Park

City Park

Oh, let's go out to City Park,
Oh, let's go out to the park.
We'll play with the fish in a
    still, blue stream,
And we won't go home until dark,
And we won't go home until dark.

Oh, let's go out to the big ball park,
Oh, let's go out to the park.
We'll get a good seat,
And we'll see a home run,
And we won't go home until dark,
And we won't go home until dark.

Oh, let's go out to the fun park.
Oh, let's go out to the park.
We'll get lost in the fun of the big
    Fun House,
And we won't go home until dark,
58   And we won't go home until dark.

Trip to the Park

We work with words.

dark   hard   far

card   cut   cook

hand   hid   pan

fall   tall   wall

map   Ben   list

hug   hot   hope

Sound the words.

park

car

band

ball

Dad

hit

Sight words.

<u>Beto</u> and <u>Sara</u> like to play ball.

59

Let's Go to the Park

"It's a good day," said Mom.

"Let's go to the park.

Let's get in the car and go."

"Yes! Yes!" said Sara.

"Let's go to the park!"

"Wait! Wait," said Dad.

"We may not get a place to park
the car."

"Then we will not take the car,"
said Mom.

60   "We can walk to the park from here."

"Look, Beto!" said Sara.

"See the boy with his dog.

See the girl make her dog jump."

"It's a dog show," said Mom.

"A dog must look good to win."

"Wait! Look what I found," said Beto.

"That brown one is a good dog.

I want it to win."

"Oh! Yes! I do, too," said Sara.

"But I don't think it's in the show."

"We'll see the dog show again," Dad said.

"But let's go to the ball game now."

"Look, Sara," said Beto.
"See them play ball.
What a hit!
It's a home run!
Was that hit just luck?"

"No! That girl is good,"
said Sara.
"She can hit that ball!"

"Look, Mom, Dad!" said Beto.
"Do you like that band, Dad?"

"Yes! What a sound!" Dad said.
"With luck that band can make it big."

"That band may not be big, but it's
62   loud," said Mom.

We work with words.   Sound the words.

bedroom   without   into   maybe

far   card   hard   dark

hope   life   paint   bike

strike   stroke   stream

Sight words.

<u>Someone</u> said my <u>sister</u> is here.

Fun in the Park

"Look, a bike stand," said Mom.

"Let's take a bike ride.

We can see the park from a bike."

63

"I want to ride to the stream,"
said Beto to his sister.

"But I want to see a bear," said
Sara.

"We can see it all on our bike trip,"
Dad said.
"Beto, ride with your sister.
I'll ride with Mom."

"That was a good ride," said Beto.

"Did you see the frog in the stream?

I like it down by the stream."

"I saw a big bear," Sara said.

"I like to see the big bear play

with the little bear in the zoo."

"Sister! Sara!" said Beto.

"Did you see that brown dog again?

It did run with us!

I still think it's a good show dog."

"So do I," said his sister.

"Soon it will be dark," said Mom.

"We must not stay in the dark.

Maybe it's time to go.

We didn't come in the car.

So let's not wait to walk home."

65

"Look! Oh, look!" Sara said.

"The little brown dog has a
blue tag!

It did win! It did!

Maybe it has no home.

May it stay with us?"

"We can take it home and I'll see
if someone lost it," Dad said.

"If someone does not want it,
maybe it can be our dog.

Now this day in the park was fun.

But soon it will be dark.

It's time to go."

Someone Who Cares

67

No Place like Home

We work with words.

vat   live   gave

winner   summer   better

Sound the words.

Eve

dinner

Sight words.

My <u>mother</u> and my <u>grandmother</u> are here.

Let's Go, Frog!

"Mother, may I go to the monster show?" said Eve.

"Not yet, Eve," said Mother.
"We must eat first.
And Grandmother wants you."

"Eve, will you get your skate off my bed?" Grandmother said.

"Eve! The dog wants to eat your frog," big sister said.
"Will you get the dog or frog?"

"Eve! Will you turn down the sound track?" said Grandmother.

"Eve! Now your frog is in the
dinner sauce," said big sister.
"Will you fish him out?"

"Stop! This is not good!" said Eve.

"Eve, don't shout at your sister
or grandmother," said Mother.
"We don't need all that noise."

Eve didn't make more noise.
She didn't wait for dinner.
She just got on her bike and went
for a ride.

"We'll show them, Frog," she said.
"We'll not stay for dinner.
And from now on, we'll just do
what we want."

Eve and Frog went up First Street,
then down the next street.

"Maybe we'll get a job with
a rock band," she said.
"Or maybe we'll hop on a train.
Maybe we can go to work on a big
oil well.
Mother did when I was little.
But first, we'll go see the
monster show."

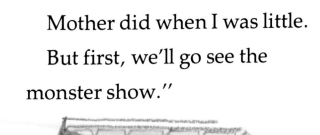

puzzle bottle pebble   middle

today lay stay   pay

hard hand hum   hug

without inside outside   into

<u>Father</u> and <u>brother</u> are home.

In the City

Eve and Frog went into the city,
street by street.

Soon they were in the middle
of the city.

But Eve didn't see the monster show.
So they went into a truck stop to eat.

"I want one egg, and so does my
friend," said Eve.

"Can you pay for it?" the woman said.

"Well, no," said Eve.

"But you must pay," the
woman said.
"And we can't let a frog eat here."

So Eve and Frog went out.

"Maybe we will not run off just yet,"
said Eve.
"Let's go home and eat first."

This way and that way, Eve and Frog
went to look for home.

"Frog," said Eve.
"I don't want to say this.
But I must.
Friend, we are lost.
We are lost in the middle
of the city."

Just then the bike had a flat.

"This is all we need," said Eve.

"We are lost in the middle of the city.

It's dark, and I see the moon.

Father and Brother are home from work by now.

And I want to be home, too!"

"Are you Eve and Frog?" said the man in blue.

"Your father and brother came to have us look for you.

They all want you at home.

Hop into our car."

Mother, Father, Grandmother, Sister,
and Brother all gave her a hug.
And a hug again! And again.
They gave Frog a hug, too.
And Eve and Frog got to eat at last.

"Well, Frog," said Eve.
"Maybe we can't do just what
we want.
But still, there is no place
like home."

No One Else like Me

Stan

Steve rest best

world worth

gave hope mail

tool takes fit

coin point soil

mark card part

Stan

worst

team

Tom

join

hard

<u>Spin</u> the top, Tom.

78

Stan, the Worst

"Stan, come and play ball," said Tom.
"Come and join our team.
We need you to play."

"I don't want to join your team,"
said Stan.
"I can't hit the ball."

"We need you, Stan," said Tom.
"Come and join our team!"

"This is not a game I can play,"
said Stan.
"But I will try this time."

"You can hit first, Stan," said Tom.

"Dig your feet into the ground."

"This is not my game," said Stan.

"But I will try to hit the ball."

"Hit a home run," they said.

"Look out! Hit the ball hard!

Oh! Look at Stan spin and hit

the ground.

Get up, Stan.

Try again to hit the ball hard."

Stan did try, again and again.

But he didn't hit it.

"All I do is spin like a top,"
said Stan.

"We don't need you now, Stan,"
said Tom.
"We don't need someone to spin
like a top.
You are the worst one on the team.
You are the worst one in this park.
You are the worst one in this city!"

"I may be the worst one," said Stan.
"But I didn't want to join this team.
This is not my game.
I'll just look at you play."

81

Stan, the Best

"I'll not play ball again," said Stan.

"I'll just sit and root for the team.

It will happen again if I try to help.

I can't hit the ball.

So all I can do is root for the team.

"I must do a better job.

I must do a better job soon.

Then this will not happen again.

I must do better!"

"That dog has our ball," said Tom.

"Can you do something to help, Stan?

Help us get our ball back.

Don't let something bad happen to it.

Stop that dog!"

"Yes. I can do something," said Stan.
"I can run fast.
It is what I do best.
It will not be hard to get the ball."

"Look at Stan run!" said Tom.
"He can run as fast as the wind."

"I have the dog now," said Stan.
"Here is your ball, Tom."

"Stan, you can run fast," said Tom.

"Yes. I did my best," said Stan.
"I may be the worst one on the team.
But I can run the best."

The Almost-Magic Machine

If You Had a Robot

We work with words.

hotel   visit   even

happy   Nelly   sunny

glory   baby   pony

Sound the words.

robot

funny

story

Sight words.

I <u>know</u> the robot <u>doesn't</u> talk.

86

Do you happen to know what a robot is?

Well, if you don't know, I'll tell you.

A robot is made by people.

It is something you can use.

A robot can be a funny toy.

87

A robot can do what
you can do.

You can make a robot so it will
stand and walk and talk.

You can make it bend and hop
and run.

But what use is a robot?

Well, it can work, work, work!

A robot doesn't have to eat
or sleep.

It doesn't take time off to rest.

And it doesn't need time for fun.

But it can be funny if you ask it
88   to be funny.

You can make a robot that will work
for you.

If you have a robot like that,
you can do what you want.

And the robot can do what
you don't want to do.

Maybe you can sleep late.

Then the robot can do
your work for you.

And you will have more time
to play.

89

Maybe you can make a robot that
will howl when you tell a funny story.

Maybe it can play ball with you.

Just think! It may hit
a home run!

You know, a robot can be a big
help and a good friend.

Or it can be funny
for you.

Maybe you can make a robot that
will read a story.

It can read this story, too.

Doesn't that sound funny?

Ben and His Robot

We work with words.

music	never	paper
able	cable	fable
Beth	cut	Dan
fit	hand	hot
gave	hope	life
hid	left	hum

Sound the words.

hotel

table

Ben

ran

ate

sat

Sight words.

Ben Franklin put the robot there.

There is a story about the
first robot in the U.S.A.

We still don't know if it's true.

It is said that Ben Franklin made
the first robot.

Ben Franklin, you ask?

Yes! The Ben Franklin.

Way back in his time, no one but Ben
had found a way to make a robot.

Ben soon found his robot to be
a friend as well as a robot.

When Ben came home from work, he
found time to play with his robot.

Ben ran with his robot.

He ate dinner at the table with it.

Then they sat at the table to talk.

Think of it!

Way back then, Ben found a way to
make the robot talk a little.

How did he do it, you ask?

We don't know.

Ben didn't say.

The robot Ben Franklin made is not with us now.

When Ben was put to rest, the robot was put in a hotel.

The hotel people had to see that the robot was fine for all time.

But one day the robot had a bad fall in the hotel.

Ben was not there to fix it.

So the first robot in the U.S.A. was lost in that fall.

Maybe you will make a robot one day.

Maybe your robot will sit as his sat.

Maybe it will eat at the table as his ate.

And run as his ran.

Your robot may talk, too.

Then we will ask you how Ben Franklin made his robot.

Tall-Tale Adventures

How I Got My Skates

We work with words.   Sound the words.

bumped looked mixed	jumped
fished howled joined	happened
ended needed sounded	landed
wished worked	rained
task skin mask	asked
washed wand	wanted
start Steve storm	rested
talked mall hall	walked
gave Steve seen	trade
baby body never	pony

I Take a Trip

One day I walked out of the house.

The sun was in the sky.

It was just the day for a little trip.

I got on my bike.

I wanted to go fast.

But the bike didn't go fast.

It came to a stop.

I jumped off it.

The bike had a flat!

What did I do?

I'll tell you what I did.

I saw a woman in a truck.
She was my big sister.
"Stop!" I said.

The truck came to a stop.
"I am on a trip," I said.
"But my bike has a flat.
May I ride with you?"

"Yes," she said.
"You may put your bike
in the back of the truck.
I must go to the next city.
You may come with me."

Let me tell you what happened next.

I put the bike in the truck.

Then I jumped in, too.

I rested in the back of the truck.

But just then we hit something.

Bump! The truck went up.

I went up, too!

Bump! The truck came down.

I came down, too!

The truck came to a stop.

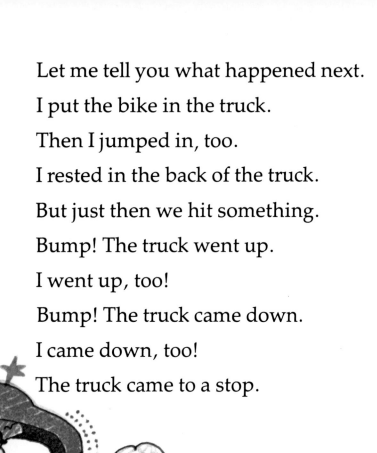

"What happened?" I asked.

"We hit a big rock," she said.
"The truck landed in a big hole.
Now it has a flat.
We can't get it out."

Just then a man came by.
He had a car.

"Can you help us?" we asked.

"Yes, but it will take time,"
he said.

We didn't want to wait.

So we made a trade, the truck for the car.

But the man wanted help to get the truck out of the hole.

So we let him ride in the car with us to get help.

I rested again.

But it didn't last.

Bump! Bump! Bump!

I jumped up to see what had happened.

We landed by the curb.

We had a flat again.

What did we do then?

We wanted something to ride in.

But the car was no good.

We had no truck.

We had no bike.

So we walked. And walked.

And walked.

Then something landed on me.

It was water from the dark sky.

"Now will it rain?"

I asked.

It did.

It rained and rained.

It rained hard.

We all ran to get under a tree.

"This is the worst trip I have made,"
I said.

"I wish we had a pony," said
the man.

"A pony does not get a flat."

That was a joke.

But it did not sound funny to me.

I wanted to go home!

"I want something to ride,"
I said.

"A pony will do."

We rested under the tree.

At last the rain came to a stop.

Soon a girl came by on skates.

"Stop! I need your skates," I said.

"I have a bike.

It is a good bike.

But it has a flat.

It is in a truck.

Go down the road and you will see
the truck in a hole.

I will trade you the bike for
your skates."

So we made a trade.

And that is how I got my skates.

Skates, Take Me Home!

I had needed a way to get home.

So I got my skates in a trade.

But I was still not home.

105

I went fast on the skates.

I didn't want to take a trip,
I just wanted to get home.

I needed to be home,
but I got too warm, so I rested.

Then I went on again.

I hit a bump and landed hard
on the curb.

Never had I landed so hard.

But I was home.

That was some trip!

I never wanted a trip like that.

I'll never take a trip like that again.

First I was on my bike.

Next I was in a truck.

Then I got in a car.

I had to walk some of the way.

Last of all, I was on skates.

Some rain came down.

And I got too warm.

But I made it home.

On the next warm day,

I'll stay home.

Or I may get a pony.

A pony is good for a trip.

It will never have a flat.

That is my story.

Is it true?

What do you think?

Make Your Own

The Last Chicken Sandwich

We work with words.

each   reach   bench

reach   bunch   ranch

chin   chain   chop

ticket   pocket

Sound the words.

beach

lunch

chips

chicken

Sight word.

May I have a <u>sandwich</u>?

110

His name is Flap Brown.

He can outrun, outtalk, outshout, and outeat all us First Street people.

But the day came when little Sue Blue Stream was on the beach, too.

We were all on the beach, see?

And it was lunch time, see?

We saw this sandwich stand.

The lunch stand man said, "All you can eat for $1.69."

So Flap said, "Let's go!"

We all had one sandwich with chips for lunch.

That is, all of us but Flap and little Sue Blue Stream.

"One more chicken sandwich and chips," said Sue.

Well, Flap didn't want Sue to top him, you know.

"One more for me, too," he said.

Now, Sue Blue Stream didn't stand for that.

"Give me more chips!" she said.

"More chips and one more chicken
sandwich," said Flap.

And the race was on.

Soon more and more people came
from the beach to see them eat.

"Just look at them eat,"
a man said.

The sandwich stand man had a funny look.

But he didn't stop them.

I think he wanted to see the show, too.

And what a show it was.

It got late.

Some people went home.

And still Sue and Flap ate.

113

"One more chicken sandwich," said
Sue as the sun went down.

"One more for me, too," Flap said.
But that last chicken sandwich did it.
He went down, too green to talk.

When he was better, Flap said,
"Well, Sue, you win.
But I'll win the next one.
Last one in the water is —"

"A chicken?" asked Sue.
"No, Flap, I have to get home.
Or I'll be late for dinner."

And that is how little Sue Blue
Stream got the best of Flap Brown.

It's Picnic Time

We work with words. Sound the words.

ring	sing	thing	bring
beam	gave	takes	hope

Sight words.

The <u>family</u> went on a <u>picnic</u>. 115

Good!

Here come some people.

They will like our place
for a family picnic.

And we like to have them
use our place for a picnic.

"What for?" you ask.

Well, we like to make a picnic
of the picnic.

We get to play a joke on them.

116   Do you want to see how we do it?

First, we will make a wish.

"I hope they bring a chicken sandwich."

"I hope they just bring something good
to eat."

"I hope they bring chips.
I like chips."

Then we wait for the people to sit down.

"Well, here we are," they say.
"It's a warm day.
The sun is out.
Just the day for a family picnic.
Let's take a walk.
Then we'll eat."

Off they go.

Now see what each of us does.

We must work as a team.

It's a big job to take a chicken
sandwich and some chips.

Let's go!

Just in time!

Here they come!

That family will not like our
picnic.

But there is some for each of them.

And there is a little for each of us.

You see, our family needs to

eat, too.

Can't Scare Me

A Bear in the Night

We work with words.   Sound the words.

dear   beard   fear   hear

earth   learn   search   heard

tear   year   ear   near

perfect   gremlin   order   window

husky   easy   happy   Ricky

Sight words.

Where is the very big bear?

120

"It's good that you can stay here for
the night, Ricky," said Ben.

"You will have fun here.
This is where you can sleep."

"It's very dark up there," said Ricky.
"How can I see where it's so dark?
Will you be near?"

"Yes, I'll be down here," said Ben.
"I'll be near you."

121

"I can't see very well," said Ricky.

"But I hear something.

I hear something very near!

Help! Ben! I see a big bear!

I hear and see a bear!"

"Where, Ricky?" Ben asked.

"I'm up here, now.

Oh! That was not a big bear you
heard and saw.

You just heard the wind blow
on the window.

You saw the moon in the window
make this toy look near and very big.

He will be your friend as you sleep.

Good night, Ricky."

Bump and Jump
in the Attic

We work with words.

Sound the words.

circle   after   doctor   gremlins

border   born   cord   order

center   ankle   contest   perfect

cut   dust   pond   Dan

been   Pete   beat   Steve

wax   Ann   Beth   hid

tool   food   choose   room

letter   ladder   Nelly   attic

Sight word.

<u>Two</u> gremlins are in the attic.

123

"What is that noise?" Dan asked.
"I can't sleep."

"It's from up there," said Steve.
"Gremlins were up there.
They may still be there.
If you see them when it is not
dark, they will do what you want."

"Is that true, Steve?" Dan asked.

"Maybe and maybe not," Steve said.
"Now will you go to sleep?"

"Dan," Mother said the next day.

"It's your turn to put this room
in perfect order.

Steve has to go with me."

"It's too hard to put this room
in perfect order," Dan said.

"I need Steve to help."

"No, I need Steve with me," Mother said.

So they went into the city.

And Dan went to work on the room.

"This work is too hard," Dan said.

"You gremlins in the attic,
come down and help me.

Do you hear me?"

Down from the attic came two gremlins, one red and one blue.

"I'm Bump and he is Jump," said the blue one.

"We heard and we'll help."

Soon the room was perfect.
The two gremlins hid again in the attic.
Then Mother and Steve came home.

"Good! How did you do it?" said Steve.

"The gremlins who hid in the attic did the work," said Dan.

"Is that true?" asked Steve.

"Maybe, and maybe not," said Dan.

Clocks and Calendars

Old and Not-So-Old Clocks

We work with words.   Sound the words.

hold   told   cold   old

clap   clean   class   clock

cloud   close   cloth   clocks

clear   dear   fear   gear

hand   hum   pin   hands

pan   send   shut   sand

freezes   mixes   places   uses

This clock uses the sun to tell time.

The sun will make a line on it.

The line will tell you what time it is.

This clock will tell you the time
of day.

But it must be in the sun to work.

This clock uses sand.

The sand at the top can run down into
a hole.

The sand will run down, little by little.

When it has all come down, you turn the
clock.

The sand will run down again.

If you see one, you will say,
"This clock uses sand."

This clock is not as old as some clocks.

It is not as old as the sand or the sun clocks.

It will work night or day.

A gear will make it run.

It has hands to show the time.

And it will make a loud noise to get you up.

Some clocks are old, and some are not.

Some clocks use a gear and hands.

Some clocks don't have a gear or hands.

But they all help us tell time.

The Big Weekend
of Joey Green

We work with words.

cold sold hold

grandfather without doghouse

that's those

code bake reach

baby visit Inez

chalk check such

helped bumped worked

Sound the words.

told

weekend

than

each

over

much

called

Sight words.

<u>Joey</u> didn't go to <u>school</u>.

131

"Let's hear it for the weekend,"
Joey said.

Joey did like the weekend.
He did like it more than chips,
and maybe more than a monster show.

"I think I'll just make each day
a weekend day," Joey said.
"There, now I can sleep late.
And play ball with Don or ride my bike
with Eve.

Let's hear it for the weekend!"

"Get up, Joey," his mother called
next day as she went to work.
"You'll be late for school."

"See? No school for me," he told her.
"I made each day a weekend day."

She didn't have time to say much as
she ran out, late for work.
"I'll ask Don to come over,"
Joey said.
"He can come over and play ball with me!
Let's hear it for the weekend."

But when Joey called, Don was not home.
He was in school.

And as he called, Joey found that Flap,
Jean, and Eve were each in school, too.

"It's not much fun," said Joey over and
over as he just sat. And sat. And sat.
So he went to sleep.

Joey heard someone come in.
His mother was home from work.

"How did you like your weekend, Joey?"
she asked.

"Not much!" Joey told her.
"Let's hear it for school!"

And Joey never made a weekend again.

MYSTERY MESSAGES

2 Big Word Lists

IN THIS ISSUE

BONUS 4 PAGE NOVEL

The End
of the
Foot Long
Hot Dog

A Little of This and That

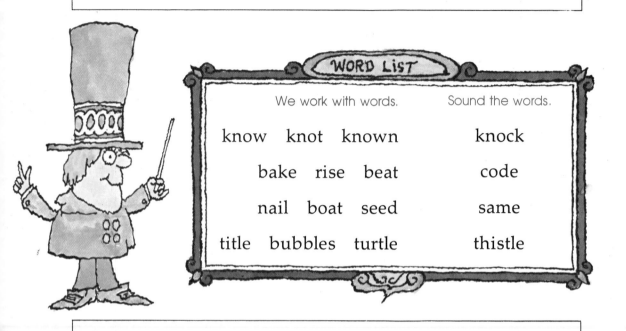

WORD LIST

We work with words.			Sound the words.
know	knot	known	knock
bake	rise	beat	code
nail	boat	seed	same
title	bubbles	turtle	thistle

Knock! Knock!

Who is it?

Thistle.

Thistle, who?

Thistle be the last knock, knock joke.

Name the Word

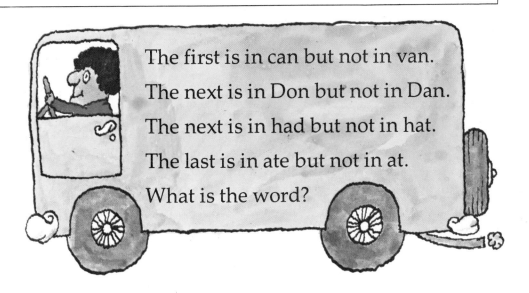

The first is in can but not in van.

The next is in Don but not in Dan.

The next is in had but not in hat.

The last is in ate but not in at.

What is the word?

Eve: What is green, can hop,
   and likes to play ball?

Ben: I don't know.

Eve: A frog.

Ben: I didn't know a frog can play ball.

Eve: It can't. I said that to make it hard.

Mom Makes a Code

One day Don came home and found a code.

12-1-10-4-14-9-3-8   9-12   9-10

13-8-5   2-11-15

"Try to read this code," said Mom.
"Then you will know where to look
for something to eat."

Can you help Don? Here is how:

1 is the same as A.

2 is the same as B.

3 is the same as C.

Here are the rest.

4-D 7-G 10-N 13-T

5-E 8-H 11-O 14-W

6-F 9-I 12-S 15-X

(Mom's code — A sandwich is in the box.)

Word List

wheel	while	white	which
	whine	whether	why
far	part	start	yard
paper	visit	ever	meter
underwater	outside	inside	cannot
sing	ring	string	thing
dollar	letter	summer	gallon
strong	sing	song	long
pet	mask	pond	hot
shut	pan	pin	hat

Soon, you must say <u>liter</u>, not gallon.

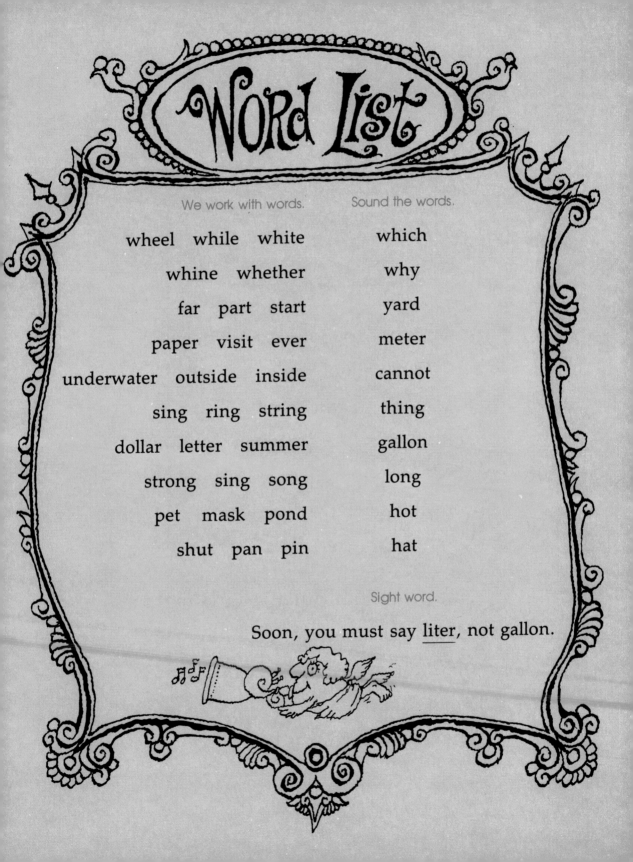

THE END OF THE FOOT-LONG HOT DOG

Which is best, a foot-long hot dog, or a 0.3048 meter hot dog?

Well, soon you will know.

For the day may come when you cannot get a foot-long hot dog to eat.

Soon you may have to order a 0.3048 meter hot dog.

Some people think that a 0.3048 meter hot dog is not as good as a foot-long hot dog.

And some people think a 0.3048 meter hot dog is fine.

Which do you think is best?

And, keep this under your hat, soon a 10-gallon hat will not be a 10-gallon hat.

Which may happen the same day there is not one more foot-long hot dog.

Why?

Why will a 10-gallon hat not be a 10-gallon hat?

I'll tell you.

It will be a 37.85 liter hat, that is why.

A 37.85 liter hat just doesn't sound the same, does it?

Soon you cannot even get a seat on the 50-yard line at a ball game.

Why not?

There may be no 50-yard line.

It will be a 45.7200 meter line.

That is just not the same thing, is it?

But meter or yard, liter or gallon, one thing will still be the same.

A chicken sandwich will still be a chicken sandwich.

It will be the same thing, as long as you don't order a foot-long sandwich.

If you do, you will have a hard time.

A Loaf of Bread

A Trip to a Shop

We work with words.

Sound the words.

looking   raining   seeing

working

telling   thinking   walking

washing

round   cloud   noun

flour

takes   looks   days

pans

choose   cartoon   fool

food

Sight word.

144

Go out that <u>door</u>.

We went on a trip to a shop.

In this shop, people use flour
to make food.

We went in the door of the shop
to see the people working.

They let us help use the flour.

Roy was working too hard.

He made the flour fly.

The people didn't make Roy stop
working.

But a man did have to get the
flour up.

We saw some people washing and washing some big pans near the door.

They were working so hard they didn't hear us.

Nan said something to a man.

It made him jump and bump the door.

He let two big pans slip.

The pans made a loud noise.

The man had to wash the pans again.

We saw people working with flour.

And we saw people washing pans.

They were all working to make food.

Do you think they will let us come back?

The Good Food Show

We work with words.

Sound the words.

breathe	beach	reach	knead
head	read	dead	bread
heavy	rainy	easy	ready
bead	leave	seal	yeast
side	mail	nail	bake
hose	music		rise
sir	hurt	stir	girls
cars	poles	adds	boys
you're	I'll	he's	we're

Sight words.

Mix the <u>salt</u> and flour <u>together</u>.

147

How do you do, girls and boys?

What good food do you think I'll make
on this show?

See if you can tell. Ready?

You can eat it at lunch or dinner.

It is good with chicken or fish.

You use it to make a sandwich.

To make it, you bake it.

What is it, boys and girls?

Yes! It's bread!

Are you ready?

Then let's make bread together.

You need flour, water, oil, and this.

And you need yeast.

Mix together the salt, flour, water,
and oil.

Put in some of this.

Now put in yeast that is in warm water.

Put in more flour.

And mix it all together again.

149

Let's see now, boys and girls.

We have put in flour, water, oil, salt, yeast, and this.

We must have in the yeast or the bread will not rise.

Now, we're to knead and knead.

We must work very hard to knead it.

Then we must wait and let the bread rise.

Next, we're to put it in the bread pans and let it rise again.

At last, we're ready to bake.

Bake it, and when it is ready, then take it out.

Did you like to see me make bread, boys and girls?

On my next show, I'll show you how to bake a fish dinner.

These Are My People

Stories of the Black Bear

We work with words.

Sound the words.

legs	bikes	books	friends
parked	showed	worked	looked
small	smart	smell	smiles
spots	plays	runs	hugs
pound	round	noun	clouds
ring	song	sang	things
	earth	earn	learn
after	until	pocket	doctor
nail	nice	own	an

Sight words.

Tell me stories about the black bear.

152

"No!!!"

"But, Ann! She is your grandmother,"
my mother said.

"My grandmother?" I said.
"Just an old woman, that is what she is!
She will be in the way."

"Ann!" said my mother.
"It is the old way of our people
to help the old when they need it."

"Our people?" I said.
"Why do you say, our people?
My people are my city friends!
Not an old woman I don't know."

153

"Ann, go to your room!" Mother said
as she looked hard at me.

And that is how it was when they said
Grandmother was to come and stay here.
But she came, my grandmother did.
She came with smiles and hugs.
She came with stories of the black bear
and stories of the sister of the moon.

But I had no smiles and hugs for her.
And I didn't want to hear stories of the
black bear or of the sister of the moon.
Was I not a city girl with city friends?
What good were these stories in the city?

So my grandmother put up her smiles, and hugs, and stories.

But still, she did try to be of help.

She got up first each day.

And with no noise, she made a good lunch for all of us to take with us.

She made bread and had it ready for us when we got home.

And she looked for clouds, and when they came over, she set out pans.

This let her wash our things in rain water from the clouds.

She never said water from the clouds was the old way to wash things.

But I knew it was and I didn't like it.

But the day came when I had to learn
a thing or two about the old way.

I had to learn about people who have
come to be old.

I had to learn about my grandmother.

It happened when I got home with my
mother and my brother from a ball game.

I didn't feel very good at all.

It was hot, but I was about to freeze.

Then at dinner, things just went black.

Next thing I knew, I was in bed, with
the family doctor over me.

"It doesn't look good," I heard the
doctor say.

Then the black came again.

They told me the rest of it when
the worst was over.

They told me how my grandmother went
out late that night, in the rain.

She didn't let my father go with her.

They told me she came back very, very
late with a green plant and a brown root.

They must have come from City Park.

But how she found them in the dark, way
over in City Park, we still don't know.

They told me how she put the root and
plant with rain water.

And how she got it down me, a little
at a time.

She was up with me all night, they
said.

When I came to, she told my family,
"I think maybe she will be fine now."

Next day, I asked, "Grandmother, will
you tell me the story of the black bear?
Or maybe the one about the sister
of the moon?"

"Well," she said, with one of her
smiles and a big hug.
"Long time back, there was the black bear.
And he came to our people to show them
who they were, and how to . . ."

ACKNOWLEDGMENTS

For permission to adapt and reprint copyrighted materials, grateful acknowledgment is made to the following publisher:

The Saturday Evening Post Company for "Ben and His Robot" adapted from "The Philadelphia Man" by Aileen Lorberg in *Jack and Jill* magazine. Copyright © 1973 by The Saturday Evening Post Company, Youth Publications, Indianapolis, Indiana.

Grateful acknowledgment is made to the following for reproduction of photographs and color transparencies on the pages indicated:

John M. Beals 57, 127, 128, 129, 130; William Bradley 47; E. Irving Eldredge 47; David Fitzgerald 151; Connie Hwang 77; Pauline L. Lane 47.

Grateful acknowledgment is made to the following for illustrations on the pages indicated:

Don Branham 135, 136, 137, 138, 139, 140, 141, 142; James Cummins 68, 69, 70, 71, 72, 73, 74, 75, 76; Pamela Frost 37, 38, 39, 40, 41, 42, 43, 44, 45, 46, 119, 120, 121, 122, 123, 124, 125, 126; Jon Goodell 7, 8, 9, 10, 11, 12, 13, 14, 85, 86, 87, 88, 89, 90, 91, 92, 93, 94; Murray McKeehan 27, 28, 29, 30, 31, 32, 33, 34, 35, 36, 95, 96, 97, 98, 99, 100, 101, 102, 103, 104, 105, 106, 107, 108, 109, 110, 111, 112, 113, 114, 115, 116, 117, 118, 131, 132, 133, 134; Carol Newsom 143, 144, 145, 146, 147, 148, 149, 150; Tom Newsom 79, 80, 81, 82, 83, 84, 152, 153, 154, 155, 156, 157, 158, 159; Sherry Thompson 15, 16, 17, 18, 19, 20, 21, 22, 23, 24, 25, 26; Jane Yamada 48, 49, 50, 51, 52, 53, 54, 55, 56; Julie F. Young 58, 59, 60, 61, 62, 63, 64, 65, 66.